Do Unto Others

What Critics Are Saying About
Do Unto Others

Note: New FCC regulations now demand that the full context of an
excerpted quote be printed along with the blurb.

"I loved . . . it."
—Darren La Verne, *Stats & Lists Monthly*
"I loved *The Full Monty*. It was a great movie."

"Do Unto Others is . . . the most important book
of all time."
—Professor Christopher McCullough, Richard Schroeder University.
"Do Unto Others is not the most important book of all time. In
fact, it may be the least important."

". . . A blast . . ."
—Reggie Pluntfarb, *Pluntfarb News*
"A literary atrocity. I'd like to spray a blast of gas all over this wretched book."

"Pure bl . . . iss."
—Todd DeHart, *GCF Magazine*
"Pure blasé pissy nonsense."

"B . . . r . . . i . . . l . . . l . . . i . . . a . . . n . . . t . . ."
—D. Lawrence Miller, *Salve Magazine*
"Bloated, retarded, idiotic, lousy, ludicrous, inane, asinine nonsense. Tuchus!"

" . . . a glorious triumph . . ."
—Pantsless Man in Alley
"I shall arise, a demon of the night, and shall reign terror upon the land, a glorious triumph for evil."

Do Unto Others

1,000 Hilarious Ways to Screw with People's Heads

Justin Heimberg
and
David Gomberg

 St. Martin's Griffin New York

Design by Heidi S. Eriksen

Library of Congress Cataloging-in-Publication Data

Gomberg, David.
    Do unto others : 1,000 hilarious ways to screw with people's heads / David Gomberg and Justin Heimberg.
        p. cm.
    ISBN 0-312-25291-9
    1. American wit and humor. I. Heimberg, Justin. II. Title.

PN6162.G59 2000
818'.5402—dc21   00-025470

10 9 8 7 6 5 4 3 2

Contents

Practice random kindness and senseless acts of beauty.
—Old Wisdom

Practice kind randomness and beautiful acts of senselessness.
—New Wisdom

Introduction

Everybody complains that there's nothing "to do" anymore.

Well, complain no more. Here are 1,000* things to do in over 50 locations and situations, from standing on an elevator to attending church to going on a first date.

Understand, these aren't particularly wise things to do. Nor are these the sort of actions meant to lift your spirits or bolster your moral character. If anything, these directives are meant to take meaning *away* from your lives. No, these "things to do" are not even vaguely profound, or socially redeeming in any way whatsoever. They are simply provided to help make your life, and in turn the world, a little bit stranger.

What we promote is not dangerous or rebellious; it is harmless. This is good, clean fun . . . mostly. Ways to spice up your life at the rather minor expense of con-

*By 1,000 we mean about 600.

fusing a few people along the way. Whether you actually try any of these is up to you. (Note: Please read disclaimer on following page!)

At the very least, we invite you to picture what it would be like to perform these absurdities. But don't race through them. Consume them slowly, like a fine bundt cake; truly take the time to envision and appreciate the glorious confusion that might ensue as you "practice kind randomness and beautiful acts of sense-lessness."

For Entertainment Purposes Only!

Sometimes you see this warning on places where it doesn't seem necessary, like a board game or a pinball machine. As if pinball can be used for other purposes. Evil purposes? Intellectual? Masturbatory?

Well, this goes for our book too: Entertainment Purposes Only. Basically, what we're saying is, don't actually do anything we say. If we don't say that, then we can get sued. But wait, we just said don't do anything we say. Illogical. If you should not do anything we say, and we say not to do anything we say, what should you do? Illogical! Does not compute! Overload. Overload. Overloaaaaad . . .

Do Unto Others

Decidedly Demented Things to Do in a Mall

A trip to the mall can be an unbearable experience. Long lines, over-friendly sales clerks, and hordes of whining children can take their toll. But malls don't have to be so grueling. There are plenty of ways to entertain yourself in these temples of consumption.

1. Go to Supercuts, ask them to "take a little off the stomach."

2. At Blockbuster, replace the movies in "staff recommendations" with low-budget drive-in movies and hardcore pornography like *Hot Resort*, *Sizzle Beach USA*, and *Ebony Humpers 6*.

3. Start scuffle in Foot Locker, try to get salesman to give you a technical.

4. At Barnes and Noble, hang out in self-help section, hit on vulnerable women.

5. Try to grate cheese using an escalator.

"Welcome to Circuit City, where service is state of the art."
—Ralph Waldo Emerson

1

6. When department-store employees spray you with perfume/cologne sample, scream "I'm melting....I'm melting....So much pain...Death is welcome..."; crumple to ground.

7. At Abercrombie & Fitch, badger other customers with lengthy explanations as to why Abercrombie is far superior to Fitch; distribute propaganda.

8. Go to Kmart, buy absurd combinations of things that arouse cashier's imagination. Examples: a) a calculator, some glue, and a jar of olives b) a hamster, a fork, and some paprika c) pack of thumbtacks, a menorah, and a bottle of vodka.

9. Offer to pay for things in a) pennies b) acorns c) "tales of adventure."

10. Set up book-signing table, claim you are Art Buchwald. If you choose, write delusional and threatening notes in book copies, e.g. "The infidels shall be quashed," "Cower to my genius," and "I shall shower nougat upon your first born."

11. Stroll through toy store with electronic "Simon" in pants, watch customers' confusion.

12. Go to TGI Friday's, order a table for two. Insist that Steve Guttenberg will be joining you; feign heartbreak when he doesn't show up.

13. Ask news shop if they have the latest edition of *Inhaler Aficionado*.

14. Try on biker shorts that are too small for you. Stand in front of mirror scrutinizing fit, often eliciting sales clerk's opinion.

15. Teach pet-store parrots to say, "I have a prehensile penis and retractable testicles."

16. Set up soap box in arcade, preach and rant about "Pinflation—the unnecessary increase in pinball scores"; blame Germans.

17. Go into Victoria's Secret, hand clerk sexy lingerie, tell her, "You look about my girlfriend's size. Could you try this on?"

18. Do the same thing, but say, "You look about my mom's size."

19. Do the same thing, but say "You look about Jack Sikma's size."

20. Go to piercing shop, ask them to pierce your pancreas.

21. At Barnes and Noble, fake like you're speed-reading Dostoyevsky at an absurd rate. Nod and chuckle occasionally.

22. Do the same, but pretend that you can comprehend the words simply by sniffing them.

23. Walk up to someone and "recognize" them as Carrie Fisher. Insist on getting an autograph.

24. Try to make mall cops laugh, as though they were members of England's Royal Guard.

25. Try to make them cry.

26. Open all jars of tennis balls, inhale fumes, tell people in a giggly slur that "Sport's Authority is so much better if you're stoned."

27. Take large, cumbersome, awkwardly shaped objects to department stores to be gift-wrapped. (Examples: stack of firewood, an inflated blow-up doll, a live mallard.)

Things to Do at McDonald's

If the mall is symbolic of the state of America, then McDonalds is its capital. Here are a few ways to make your Happy Meal even happier.

1. Try to get pickle slices to stick on ceiling in patterns of constellations.

2. Tell cashier you are sexually attracted to Grimace, bashfully ask if he/she could set you up.

3. At the drive-thru, ask for a) a Slurpee b) some buttermilk and sprinkles c) information regarding the whereabouts of "the General."

4. Recite in monotone, with glazed eyes, "Two all beef patties, special sauce, lettuce, cheese, pickle, onion, on a sesame seed bun. Must kill president."

5. Narrate actions like superhero. "Must get fry . . . dip in ketchup . . . distribute evenly . . ."

Perhaps the most stressful and demeaning part of the whole "getting a job" thing is the infamous job interview. Keeping in mind that not all of us can make a living writing these read-it-and-wipe gimmick books, we have provided a few ways to "maintain your dignity" during that inevitably trying ordeal. If things aren't going well, or if you suddenly realize that you are violently unqualified, then why not at least have a little fun with the interview? Why should you be the only one who is uncomfortable?

1. When interviewer goes to shake your hand, suddenly pull it away, rub through hair, and slyly say, "Psych."

2. Use the term "apeshit" as much as possible.

3. Wear acids washed jeans.

4. Converse in a) a heavy Cockney accent b) semaphore, (flags) c) several sharp blows to the stomach which vary in power and location.

"Everybody's workin' for the weekend."
—William Shakespeare

5. In the middle of a sentence, gasp in trailing voice, "Feeling sleepy . . . Must get antidote . . . Need-anti . . ."; then fall unconscious.

6. Quote Rommel a little too often.

7. Submit resume and personal essay in haiku.

8. If he/she gives you anything to read, immediately consume it.

9. If they ask, "So where are you from?" You answer, "I'm probably the creation of some insane wizard."

10. Yawn into hand, plunge hand into pocket and say, "I'll save that for later."

11. Ask interviewer to join you in a duet of "Summer Lovin' ". If he/she refuses, do both parts.

12. Periodically take off your shoes and smell your feet.

13. On job application, under criminal record, write: Arrested for a) indecent display of plaid b) obscene use of an overhead projector c) stalking the Golden Girls.

14. Act out Robert De Niro's famous "Are you talking to me?" scene from '*Taxi Driver*.'

15. Act out Sharon Stone's infamous leg-crossing scene from '*Basic Instinct*.'

16. Act out Michael J. Fox's obscure basketball scene from '*Teen Wolf*.'

17. If they ask, "What are your hobbies?" You answer a) cabbage stacking b) ghost-writing hate mail to midgets c) summer: sorcery; winter: indoor sorcery.

18. Avoid eye contact; invariably stare at his/her a) hair b) chin c) left hand d) crotch.

19. Turn armchair around, straddle it casually.

20. Talc.

21. Tell interviewer to "hold on a second," then pull out a mini-corder and say softly into it: "Idea for story. Tightass corporate type falls for unqualified interviewee. . . ."

22. Answer all questions in interpretive dance.

23. When he/she first addresses you, say, "That's my name, don't wear it out!"; chortle uproariously.

24. If they ask, "Why do you think you're qualified for this job?" You answer by a) unzipping your pants b) placing a two-pound lobster on the desk c) saying "Uh ... right ... credentials," looking around with a nervous smile, and then diving out the window.

25. When interviewer isn't looking, quickly swap his/her family photos with pictures of the cast of '*Good Times*.'

26. Enter to Tone Loc's "Wild Thing." Initiate suggestive grind with the interviewer, if you so desire, add narration such as "Dat's it. Bump n' grind ... real slow."

27. Try to always return conversation to *Joanie Loves Chachi*. For example, "Yes that's very interesting about the investment strategy, but if I might cite an episode of *Joanie Loves Chachi* ..."

28. Relentlessly bitch about how the Belgians are taking all our jobs.

29. Call interviewer "Daddio."

30. Inform interviewer that your personal statement is written on your inner thighs.

31. Consume a half dozen jalapeños before the interview. Wear long underwear and several layers of clothes and do anything you can to induce as much sweating as possible.

Being at the bottom of the corporate food chain isn't the only place to have fun. Here's yet another chapter on the subject of effective management, "effective" being the operative word.

1. Institute "Casual Friday," "Hot Pants Thursday," and "Pimp-garb Tuesday."

2. Wear a monocle.

3. Wear two monocles.

4. Wear sixteen–seventeen monocles.

5. Post huge Big Brother-like photos of yourself on all walls.

6. Post huge Big Brother-like photos of Wilfred Brimley on all walls.

7. Spend most hours of the day working on Cab Calloway impression. Get worse each day. Need encouragement.

8. Stock the supply closet with mysterious smoking boxes, canned ham, and unpackaged rice.

9. Hire team of people to dress up like Elijah Mohammed's bodyguards and form a protective phalanx around you. Have them shout things like "Tell it!" and "What he said!" after each of your comments during a presentation.

10. Wear white gloves, strike a permanently frantic expression, and mutter ceaselessly about "The germs! The evil germs!"

11. Make employees put their heads down as punishment like teachers used to do in school.

12. Have centralized radio playing the same thing all day long: a) Iron Maiden b) a tape of a wet hacking cough c) Maoist propaganda speeches.

According to senator Paul Simon, there are fifty ways to leave your lover: "Slip out the back, Jack; make a new plan, Stan; use effective rhetoric, Frederick; hitch a ride on a blimp, Jim(p); etc. And when you don't restrict yourself to methods that rhyme with your name, there are plenty more ways to get rid of that special someone who isn't that special anymore. All you need to do is develop a charming little quirk, predilection, or peeve.

1. Become all-consumed with building a perpetual-motion machine, explode in a fury when she/he questions your new "hobby."

2. In the heat of passion, accidentally call her "Mary Lou Retton."

3. Develop an offensive and irrational prejudice against the Dutch. Be vocal about it in public places.

4. Anniversary gift? One of those big foam hands that says "You're # 1."

"Love Hurts. Oooh, Oooh, Love huuuuurts."
—Alexander Pope

15

5. Develop new terms of endearment: "Schnookyballs," "Ass-face 3," "Mein Führer," and "My Loyal Minion."

6. Regularly omit the "rinse" portion of the "lather, rinse, repeat" shampoo sequence.

7. Constant off-key serenades of Gloria Estefan's "Conga."

8. Talk openly about your fantasies: a) a three-way with Adrian Dantley (all of you wearing nothing but knee-high tube socks) b) watching her/him fondle a tortoise c) a Donkey Punch from the Phillie Phanatic.

9. Insist on new homemade birth control: An English muffin with several strands of Scotch tape radiating from the center.

10. Erect a candle-lit shrine to Alan Thicke. Casually refer to him as the "Greater Power."

11. If she asks, do you love me?" You answer: a) I love the idea of you b) I love your genitals c) I love the way I am with you. And without you. d) I love me. I am great!

12. Get a full torso tattoo of a) Mel Torme b) the quadratic formula c) your inner organs.

13. Administer Rogaine to nipples and palms.

14. Three words: wet hacking cough.

15. Three more words: Ralph Sampson fetish.

16. Seven more words: construct a lamp shade of pubic hair.

17. Tirelessly propose romantic ground-beef baths.

18. Tell her/him that he/she's not dating you but rather "Jesus through you."

19. Keep getting her confused with former Baltimore Oriole Lenn Sakata. As in "Were you the one I had dinner with last night or the versatile utility man for the 1983 World Series team?"

20. Start to leave out a) empty liquor bottles b) hamsters c) *Plumpers Magazine* d) a molted skin shell of yourself.

21. Give up utensils for "religious reasons."

22. Nickname your penis.

23. Nickname other people's penises.

24. Fake orgasm. (On the subway.)

25. Find an "old favorite" shirt, a lime green tee that says "I said *sit* on my face!" with a picture of a woman defecating on a man's face to his horror/frustration.

26. Insist on all vacations in a) Meade, Kansas b) your neighbor's yard c) your favorite shirt.

27. Become inexplicably irate at the sight of toast.

28. Leave the toothpaste cap off (and covered with blood).

29. Leave the toilet seat up (and covered with blood).

30. Alter your musical tastes from soft contemporary pop to violently loud ancient Gaelic ritual chants.

31. Tell her you're attracted to both her parents.

32. New cologne/perfume preference: zesty salsa.

Things to Do When Meeting the In-Laws for the First Time

If none of those work, there are chances down the line to ruin a relationship . . .

1. Act disinterested in anything one of them has to say, and enthralled with the other. When the "boring" one speaks, make the yapping gesture with your hand and/or break into the theme song from *All in the Family*.

2. Offer housewarming gift: a) a live goose b) the deed to a fictional ranch in Montana c) eight empty milk cartons on a piece of twine (offer no explanation of what this is).

3. Demand a dowry, laugh with them as if you all think it's a joke. Then reiterate, "No seriously, where's the dowry?"

4. Nod politely as you are told something and then say, "That's interesting, uh . . ." And then double barrel middle fingers at the speaker.

5. Use the phrase "skull-fuck" more than one might expect. Use it as various parts of speech.

4

Beautifully Blasphemous Things to Do in Church

Whether your denomination be Catholic (the religion of guilt), Protestant (the religion of repression), or Unitarian Universalist (the religion of arts and crafts), church has one thing in common: It's boring. But you can do something about it. In fact, there are many things you can do about it. True, some of these things may not be in the best of taste, and if it turns out that religion is actually important, heaven's bouncer, St. Peter, is going to kick your irreverent ass right out of the Pearly Gates and you may be looking at some serious purgatory. But hey . . . God is supposed to be forgiving, right?

"Maybe we're wrong about this whole God thing."
—John 8:15

1. Ask priest for low-fat communion wafer.

2. Giggle like a schoolgirl any time the priest or minister mentions moral "duty."

3. Inflate/pass out presermon beach ball.

4. Replace organ music with "We're Not Gonna Take It" by Twisted Sister.

5. Fart, claim it wasn't you, but rather "Jesus working through you."

6. Pencil in a "Malone" next to each "Moses" in the Bible.

7. After minister quotes from the Bible, say in real sarcastic tone, "Yeah, right." Or "I'm sure."

8. Mispronounce "God."

9. Ask person sitting next to you, "How many hit points do you think Jesus had?"

10. Claim you have found God, then bring in a shackled Nipsy Russel.

11. Human beat-box during hymns.

12. Quote fake Bible passages (e.g. "There are no time-outs in the world of professional wrestling"—Shemp 3:23).

13. Start the wave.

14. Shout out to choir "Do 'Free Bird,' do 'Stairway to Heaven,'" act like this joke is the most original and brilliant thing any

one has ever done, then realize how trite it is, hide face in shame; move to the forest, adhering together a home from strewn malt-liquor cans and your own bile.

15. Use rosary beads like Mardi Gras beads.

16. Claim you are the second coming of the messiah, then perform second-rate magic tricks to prove it.

17. Startle priest with bizarre confessions: a) impure thoughts about Wolf Blitzer b) bad spelling c) maligning Dwight Eisenhower to a moose.

18. Stage-dive.

19. Exhale a tired "When is the friggin' monologue gonna be over?"

20. Replace Bibles with copies of Manute Bol's biography.

21. Call minister a) Rabbi b) Your Honor c) Mr. Roboto.

22. After minister concludes sermon, yell out a scornful, "What do you want, a biscuit?"

23. Wear uncomfortably revealing jean shorts.

24. Sneak into confession booth, pose as priest, tell penitent to do three Hail Marys, ten Rosaries, fifteen push-ups, and to watch the *Cannonball Run* movies twice in a row.

And because we are an equal opportunity offender . . .
Irresistibly Irreverent Things to Do in Synagogue

1. Give *Married With Children* hoots and hollers when your favorite Old Testament characters are mentioned.

2. Read the haftarah in the voice of Sammy Davis Jr.

3. Read Bible, giggle. Pepper with "That crazy Isaac."

4. Remind congregation "I" before "E" except after "C" and when used in Jewish surnames.

Our nation's education system is falling apart. According to a 1999 poll, fifty-eight percent of American high school students thought the Missouri Compromise was an NBA expansion team. Sixty-five percent misidentified the lyrics to "Eye of the Tiger" as the preamble to the Constitution. Twenty-seven percent claimed Michael J. Fox was president. Seventy-six percent claimed he should be. Face it. It's a lost cause. So if you're currently a student, accept the fact that you're not gonna get that B.A. Baracus in theoretical physics, and have a little fun with failure.

"School's Out for Summer! School's Out for Ever!"
—Spiro Agnew

17 Things to Do During Class

1. Ask "Is this going to be on the test?" twenty to twenty-five times a day, including after the teacher says "good morning," "good-bye," tells personal anecdotes, or sneezes.

2. Perform dramatic *Dead Poet Society* routine, where you stand on our desk and exclaim with solemn

defiance, "O captain, my captain." Look around embarrassed when no one follows.

3. Write ridiculous thesis projects: "Scott Baio and the Western World," "Gay/Lesbian Interpretations of the Smurfs," "Asner: Postmodern Perspectives."

4. In large lecture, hold up a poster that says in large letters "John 3:16."

5. Address the professor as "My Liege."

6. Cite exclusively issues of *Archie* comic books and *Swank Magazine* as resources in all of your bibliographies.

7. Pretend to be a foreign-exchange student from a fictional country. Have a translator next to you speaking loud, distracting gibberish.

8. Bestow the teacher with various nonapple fruits of appreciation: melons, 'loupes and 'dews.

9. Contemplate the fact that the sun is just an unsustainable fusion reactor destined to burn out.

10. Purposely get caught passing note around. Have the note just say "Pouridge" over and over.

11. Let nosey neighbors see your doodle: a stick figure that says "Mommy" being flogged by two midgets while a donkey watches with a big smile on his face. All of this in a thought bubble of a fish. Or Ray Liota ♥'s (your name) thousands of times in strange tiny writing.

12. Open desk drawer, whisper into it, "Soon you will all be free!"

13. After the teacher makes a point, voice indignantly, "The Germans have gotten to you too, huh?"

14. Two words: Protractor earrings.

15. In the middle of the lecture, beam a red rubber ball at your teacher. Then stand up and say, I'm sorry, I must be in the wrong class.

16. Raise hand and ask, "Could you repeat that? I was a) mentally reliving my brief stint as a cat burglar, b) fantasizing about Jeff Lebo, c) sorting various Sasquatch theories.

17. If teacher says, "Are there any questions?" you say a) Are you a good witch or a bad witch? b) Do you believe in miracles? c) Have you seen my pants? Then, stand up pantsless.

12 Things to Do on a Test That Doesn't Matter

1. Take test in a) lip balm b) blood c) a wet suit.

2. Answer every question, "former Postmaster General Marvin T. Runyon."

3. Wrap large whitefish in the test and hand it back to teacher; assure him with a confident, warm smile, "there you go."

4. Label biology diagram in "appropriate" parts—milk, milk, lemonade, round the corner, fudge is made.

5. Take the test without an internal monologue.

6. Answer question one with "see question Four." Answer question Four with "see question seven." Lead the teacher on a series of "see question"s ending with "by the time you have read this, she will already be dead."

7. Attach "notes of your work": transcripts of *Nightline*, Xeroxed photographs of professional wrestlers, and a fabricated Abraham Lincoln suicide note.

8. Two words: bagpipe breaks.

9. Color entire test in black crayon with the word "help" written in scissors scratches.

10. Employ circumlocutory proofs and reasoning that require numerous references to Freddy Mercury.

11. As you get a copy of the exam, run out screaming in a German accent, "Simon, we have da plans!"

12. Answer every question in the form of a question.

5 Things to Do on a Term Paper

1. Drop a smudge of unidentifiable thick liquid on paper. From that point on, write everything backward.

2. Put quotes around words for no reason, giving them a double entendre that doesn't "exist."

3. Forego rigid five-paragraph thesis for a) diorama b) horrid trumpet solo regarding "how the subject made you feel" c) collage of magazine photos of men in briefs.

4. Have a written lisp.

5. Blatantly attempt to lengthen your paper by giving it poetry-like margins, triple-spacing it, employing the "paragraph ending with one word on a line" trick, and heading the paper with your name, the date, class, astronomical sign, mood, Dungeons and Dragons statistics, measurements, and opinion of Bryant Gumbel.

6 Things to Do in a Debate

1. Parry insightful comments with defiant, "Talk to the hand." Escalate to, "Talk to the fist 'cause the hand is pissed."

2. Have Ed McMahon-like sidekick corroborating your assertions with a guttural, "You are correct, sir."

3. Wear breakaway pants. If you win a point of argument, rip them off triumphantly.

4. Claim song lyrics as original debate. Deliver with intense sincerity. Examples: "There comes a time when we must hear a certain call, and the world must come together as one." Or "I want to rock and roll all night and party ev-e-ry day."

5. Unsheathe irrelevant evidence to back up your point: a cage of crabs, a packet of beef jerky, a photo of Franco Harris.

6. Make the "he's been drinking" sign and point while opponent speaks. Preface your rebuttals with "That's the liquor talking."

Just because you grow up doesn't mean the fun is over.

1. Wear a black cape and demand students call you "the Maestro."

2. During lectures, without warning, shine a powerful flashlight in random students' faces and forcefully demand the correct answer.

3. Illegalize the use of the letter "R."

4. Have chalk stains all over your crotch. Pretend to be oblivious.

5. Occasionally look up and cower as if you think the ceiling is going to collapse. Do this every few minutes. Gather yourself and continue speaking.

6. When grading papers, write "Whatcha talkin' about Willis?" near rambling nonsensical answers. Write "Whoomp, there it is!" by impressive responses.

7. Assign readings of the labels of Pert Plus, Prell, and "excerpts from Head and Shoulders."

8. Put fake disturbed children's drawings up on Back to School Night.

Splendidly Strange Things to Do in an Elevator

Of all awkward experiences, there are few to rival that of an elevator ride. Standing around in a box with a bunch of strangers can be pretty uncomfortable. Why not make it more so?

> *"Love in an elevator, taking me up when I'm going down."*
> —Walt Whitman

1. Read Family Circus comics, laugh hysterically.

2. Attempt to start chant of "U.S.A.! U.S.A.!"

3. Scatter birdseed on floor. Upon receiving quizzical looks, assure them with gentle smile and say, "For Pepe."

4. Look at person, then scribble notes furiously. Repeat sporadically.

5. When someone enters, act like you are coming to, and shout deliriously, "Where's my piccolo?"

6. Enter out of breath. Ask people if they are "Milton," if they know where you can find him. Leave at the next floor, swearing.

7. Sit down.

8. Lie down.

9. Get down.

10. Wear a silver vest and sombrero. When others enter, cry, "Where's your uniform?!"

11. As you exit, dive out Indiana Jones-style, then retrieve hat just in time.

12. Read aloud from a) the Koran b) *Lady Chatterly's Lover* c) *Would You Rather...?*

13. As each new person gets on, chant in robotic drone: "Intruder alert! Intruder alert!" (Note: If you get this, you are a dork.)

14. Recite bawdy limericks, giggle mischievously.

15. Initiate a) staring contest b) slam dance c) "pile-on."

16. If they ask, "what floor?" You answer: a) "Alkanar, 7th Plane of the Underworld," b) "I don't perceive in three dimensions," c) "Where's the party?" Then dry-heave.

17. Two words: balloon animals.

18. Two more words: pork animals.

19. Start a game of Hacky Sack. Laugh at others' mistakes. Be arrogant.

20. Allude to the Bible an uncomfortable number of times.

21. Matter-of-factly take off your sock. Put in wallet. Smile warmly.

22. Look at ceiling, see if others follow.

23. Translate other people's conversations into Spanish.

24. As person exits, whisper "I love you" just as doors shut.

25. Orbit the largest guy.

26. Air guitar to elevator music.

27. Air trombone.

28. Show strangers a hair of unknown origin. Ask if they can tell you which part of your body it came from.

29. Encourage others to get off at your floor by saying, "Hurry, the rich men in zeppelins will soon be by!"

30. Stare at your palm. Say, "I think it's changing."

5

Things to Do at the Department of Motor Vehicles

1. Have sexual apparatus strewn about the backseat of your car as you conduct driving test.

2. When you are reading for the eye test, announce "P . . . O . . . R . . . N . . . O . . . hey, what kind of an eye test is this?!"

3. As you buckle in for driving test, pull out frozen fish sticks and place them on the dash. State, "I never go anywhere without these guys." Call one of the fish sticks Francis and scold him repeatedly throughout the test.

4. After successfully parallel parking, crack a beer out of the glove box. Tell evaluator that parallel parking is a "real bitch."

5. Equipment: a melon and a folding chair. Put the melon in line, then casually saunter over to your folding chair and visibly relax. Periodically ask the person behind your proxy to "please advance the melon."

"Baby, you can drive my car."
—Deborah Norville

6

Absolutely Asinine Things to Do in Places of Amusement

Our culture's sources of amusement are generally, when it comes down to it, not that amusing. Whether it's a movie about a hard-nosed cop paired with a wise-cracking squid or a swim at a beach studded with syringes and old Rolling Rock cans, leisure time activities these days leave a lot to be desired. But then again, things are what we bring to them.

"Everybody have fun tonight/ Everybody Wang-Chung tonight."
—Lord Byron

5 Things to Do at a Strip Joint

1. Tip with bologna.

2. On the juke box, select unerotic, undanceable music for the strippers to dance to. Examples: "My Way," "The Wheels On the Bus Go Round and Round," the theme to "Maude."

3. Ask the strippers if they can make change for your dollar.

4. Try to determine which river basin strippers' stretch marks resemble.

43

5. Yell a) "Mom, how could you?!" and start sobbing b) "Those are my pants!" and start sobbing c) "Bill Bixby is no more!" and start sobbing.

4 Things to Do at the Zoo

1. Play "Name that Feces."

2. Talk to chimps as if you're visiting a loved one in prison.

3. Bring small cage with exotic animal (a head of lettuce with pipe cleaner eyestalks) Call it the "Vortoosk of Cincinatti."

4. Feed the animals a) laxatives b) other animals c) to Larry Csonka.

1 Thing to Do When Visiting an Amish Farm

1. Put taffy in butter churn.

6 Things to Do on a Beach

1. Act like you're digging for sand crabs, then pull out a kitten.

2. Make sand sculpture of Bea Arthur, demand payment from any whose eyes fall upon it.

3. Put suntan oil on self or sleeping sunbather so tan-pattern says "Eddie Albert Rules!" or "Depp '04."

4. Scream with youthful enthusiasm "Seniors 2000!" Storm toward the beach, then trip and tumble. Feign severe injury.

5. Set up vending booth with "Refreshing Treats" billboarded above it. Offer only warm vodka, nuts in mayonnaise, hard-boiled eggs, saltines, and jars of paprika to be eaten like Pez.

6. Amass a mob and pick up lifeguard's chair. Sing "Hava Nagila."

10 Things to Do at Museums

1. Bring own sketch to Guggenheim Museum, put on floor, then tell guard, "I think this fell down."

2. At modern art museum, admire coatrack or museum map with knowing nods, see if others follow.

3. Put $9.99 price tags on Picassos.

4. Look at painting, turn to others and say in an irritated tone, "I can do that." Repeat with every painting in museum.

5. Lead fake tour, completely fabricating ideas; e.g. "Warhol painted this self-portrait for his lover, Bob Cousy," or "The ibex is found only in Detroit, survives on a diet of matzo-ball soup, and makes a strange mating call that sounds like 'Yahtzee.'"

6. Convince onlookers that a Jackson Pollock painting is actually 3-D Magic Art and if they stare long enough an image will appear. Feel perverted amusement at their fruitless struggle.

7. Scratch and sniff impressionist paintings.

8. At wax museum, resculpt Princess Diana's face so that she looks like Kurt Rambis.

9. Add anachronistic objects to exhibits, e.g. Big Gulps for cavemen, a Rubik's Cube in a frontier cabin, shirt that says "If you're not wasted, the day is" on a mannequin in Mount Vernon.

10. Change positions of stuffed animal nature displays to more "indecent" situations.

6 Things to Do When Playing Golf

1. Bury yourself in a sand trap garbed in a Union uniform with a note from 1845 and a bottle of old brandy.

2. Scatter Ping-Pong balls all over the fairway.

3. Have your caddy a) wheel you around in a rickshaw b) lead you on a burro c) carry you while a radio blasts "Love Lifts Us Up Where We Belong."

4. (Insert own ball-washer joke here.)

5. Walk around course, downtrodden and defeated. Lament, "This course sucks. The other one had windmills and a big ostrich pecking at the ground."

6. Militantly advocate Fred Couples.

4 Things to Do at a Scrabble Tournament

1. Insist every word has a silent "K." Challenge your opponent on this axiom every turn, acting just as surprised each time you realize your folly. Claim the dictionary is old or British.

2. Gradually eat all the vowels.

3. Play increasingly dubious words: "feltwad," "koopest," "fudgeball."

4. Talk shit. "What's up? Gotta trade in a 'Q?' He's all dressed up but nowhere to go. 'Cause I got the 'U's." Or "Who wants a hundred-tile whoop-ass?"

5 Things to Do at a Club/Bar

1. Order fake drinks such as a "Bloated Pilgrim", a "Limbless Mime", and a "Compromising Marxist". Feign rage or hurt when the bartender shamefully admits ignorance.

2. Order fake drinks, but this time explain the ingredients (e.g. a "A Cleft Foot" is a cup of lemons with vodka, grenadine, and cashews, garnished with a photograph of C. Thomas Howell).

3. Ask for drugs with non-existent nicknames: "Yo, you got any fishtails? Any baconbits?" Use college nicknames: "Razorbacks, Terps, Hoyas, Fighting Irish."

4. Send over a bowl of olives to a group of ladies. Offer a sly wink as they get them.

5. Lament pseudo-drunkenly about how nobody appreciates shoehorns anymore.

5 Things to Do with Larry

1. Take Larry to the supermarket.

2. Call Larry late at night. When he picks up phone, ask for Barry.

3. When you meet other people named Larry, ask if they are related.

4. Physically intimidate Larry.

5. Constantly insist that he's not the same Larry he used to be.

Wonderfully Warped Things to Do at a Gym/Health Club

Working out not working out? Well, if you want results, you need to work for them, don't you? Why bother? Why not use your time in the gym for far less useful purposes? And how 'bout we stop asking rhetorical questions?

"Let's get physical/I want to get physical."
—Albert Camus

1. Lay slabs of beef on sauna rocks.

2. Work out in Underoos.

3. Spot intense weightlifters and discourage effort. "Don't worry about it, don't strain. You don't have to prove anything."

4. Swim with knee pads.

5. Double up on a treadmill.

6. Demonstrate your new "exercise": arms outstretched, palms out, rigid lock-kneed high kicks.

7. Workout music: "Ride of the Valkyries," full volume.

8. Melon-eating music: "Let's Hear It for the Boy," full volume.

9. Mistake Coke machine for exercise equipment. Attempt to use the machine in every conceivable way. Exasperated, finally tell others it is out of order.

10. Try to deduce images in sweat stains on fat men's shirts, as in a Rorschach inkblot test.

11. Encourage lifters to let "Jesus lift through them."

12. When asked to show your membership card . . . show a Mark Eaton rookie card (1979).

13. Crack walnuts in Nautilus machine.

14. Tell ghost stories in steam room.

15. Put up picture of Father Guido Sarducci on the wall. Do sit-ups, lightly touching your lips to the picture as you crest your sit-up.

16. Constantly explain to huge muscle dudes that they're "doing it all wrong."

17. Work out muscles on only one side of your body until you are massively asymmetrical.

18. Run in place.

19. Gallop in place.

20. Perform violent humping motion in place.

21. Return ludicrous items to the Lost and Found: a sack of barley, a *Silver Spoons* lunch box, a spork, a retainer, etc.

22. Eye barbell menacingly. Strike yourself in the chest, crank neck, and exhale forcefully to psyche yourself up. Do this for forty straight minutes and then walk away.

23. Wear tight spandex shorts and insert any of the following objects into the crotch: a) a hammer b) a Barbie doll c) banana bunch. Wink at the ladies.

24. While on treadmill, wonder if Amish people ever "get jiggy with it."

25. Tell employee your clothes were stolen. When asked what they look like, describe exactly what they're wearing.

Things to Do in a Public Bathroom

As much of a social scene as the gym has become, the public bathrooms therein are places where people like to stick to themselves. It's a ripe time to prey on others' jitters. (Note: Voted "Worst Segue" 1999, *Transitions Magazine*)

1. At urinals, start conversations with strangers. Be a little too friendly.

2. Flush, walk out of stall with arms raised in triumph. Sing Queen song of your choice.

3. Stand slightly too far away from the urinal.

4. Stand preposterously too far away from the urinal.

5. Leave a black-and-white photo of C. Everett Koop floating in the toilet bowl.

"No paper, no paper at all/ No paper, what's my call?"
—Ken Goodson

6. In stall, after flushing, holler, a) "Oh no, my ring!" b) "Oh no, my glasses!" c) "Free at Last! Free at Last! Thank God Almighty, We're Free at Last!"

7. As you exit stall, comment, "Darn, I got it on my hands," display hand covered in sparkles.

8. Turn to guy at urinal beside you and ask, "Weren't you the big Russian in *Rocky IV*?"

9. Write odd graffiti on the wall like, "Melvin Will Return!" or "For a talented warlock, call Billy 555-9199."

10. Fill paper towel dispenser with torn out pages from Brian Bosworth's autobiography, *The Boz*.

Decidedly Disconcerting Things to Do to Freak Out a New Roommate

Not happy with your roommate? Does he leave his dirty clothes on your bed? Does she use your things without asking? Does he sit on your shirt so you have to iron it on a chair and then the fabric burns off onto the shirt and it's ruined and you have nothing to wear for the party and everybody laughs at you because all you could find was an old OP shirt, so you have to transfer to a small junior college in rural Tennessee ... uh ... we mean ... Here are a few idiosyncracies to develop if you need to freak out your roommate.

"Hell is other people."
—Darryl "Chocolate Thunder" Dawkins

1. Give your arm a hickey, adding one each successive day. Say you're getting a disease.

2. In roommate's presence, cook only one meal: a lime in the toaster.

3. Stock the refrigerator with three hundred sticks of butter. Quickly change the subject any time he/she mentions it.

4. Feign masturbation to: a) an old photograph of the "Where's the beef?" lady b) Fozzy Bear c) a poorly drawn crayon picture of your roommate d) a biography of Harriet Tubman.

5. Wear one color: periwinkle. Perhaps you are nicknamed Dr. Periwinkle. Perhaps you demand to be addressed as such.

6. Mutter in sleep a)"Must kill all humans" b)"Do it to me, Regis!" c) in the voice of Edward G. Robinson.

7. Blast NPR full volume, headbang.

8. Put up numerous posters of science fiction author, Ray Bradbury, one framed in a heart.

9. At a point when you know your roommate isn't around, call leaving absurd/ambiguous answering-machine messages to yourself in different voices. Examples: (Polite) "Hi, your robot is ready." (Fed up) "Return my helmet. This is getting ridiculous." (Panicked) "The sherbert has fermented. I repeat the sherbert has fermented. Action needed."

10. Replace all lights with orange bulbs, tell him it's "necessary for your condition." Same with the twenty-four hours a day of polka music, your Hanson sheets, and the mutual massages.

11. Answer the phone, "I am the vindicator of the damned." End with, "I wish you good tidings."

12. Stack bookshelf with twenty identical copies of a) *The Dungeons and Dragons Monster Manual* b) *The Art of Homemade Weaponry* c) Atlantic salmon.

13. Sleep between mattress and box spring.

14. Use toothpaste for all hygiene purposes.

15. Recycle jokes over and over.

16. Set up an aquarium filled with dead mammals. Feed them every day.

17. Turn over all of your furniture for "feng shui purposes."

18. As you both go to sleep ask him what you consider to be deep philosophical questions like, "Is there really a difference between lamps and the smell of cedar?"

19. Constantly grab the air around you as if you are walking through cobwebs. Suspect roommates involvement with a paranoid stare.

20. Watch TV marathons of *Who's the Boss*, recite from memory all of Alyssa Milano's lines in a spooky monotone.

21. Steal roommate's socks. Stockpile them in closet throughout semester. Return them last day of semester. Offer no explanation.

22. Put headphones on your roommate while he/she is sleeping, and subliminally teach him/her: a) to speak Russian b) titles of Ron Jeremy's complete works c) to have a fervent hatred of Redcoats.

23. Use his/her deodorant. As a popsicle.

24. Neatly organize your drawers: shirts, pants, underwear, socks, and green beans.

25. Leave odd things drying over the shower rod like bacon, a wedding dress, or damp pieces of paper that read "Rectangles amuse Gino."

26. Put a velvet rope in front of your door. Be discretionary as to admittance. Only let your roommate in if he's got chicks with him.

27. Preferred mode of transportation? Wheelbarrow.

28. When you enter the room, always reek of alcohol and have dirt on your shirt, and bloody knuckles. Tell roommate you were at the library. If he looks the least bit incredulous, repeat "At the library!"

Brilliantly Baffling Things to Do at the Office If You Just Don't Give a Crap Anymore

Every day it's the same old routine. Wake up at some ungodly hour. Read the news about the strangest murders of the previous day, and then it's straight to the office where you sweat and bleed—and for what? So the Man can buy some 800-dollar heated recliner at The Sharper Image. We get sick in the stomach just writing about it. You gotta get out, and you gotta do it with style.

"Workin' 9 to 5/ What a way to make a living . . ."
—Welp Klorp III

1. Attempt to fax bologna. Act nonplussed as the machine breaks.

2. Write all memos in pig latin.

3. Insist on getting time off for all religious holidays (i.e. Easter, Yom Kippur, Kwanza) on grounds that "you want to be covered in case one of these religions is right."

4. CC all memos to "our lord and savior who sees all."

5. CC all memos to "Craig Stadler, our lord and savior who sees all."

6. Place stickers on keyboards rearranging the letter formations. Have the mismatched letters correspond so common words spell profanity.

7. Critically compare boss's leadership abilities to Gandalf's. E.g. "Gandalf would collate psionically."

8. Fill coworkers desk with absurd combinations of things: a wrench, a condom, a cantaloupe, a dandelion, a hypodermic needle, etc.

9. Spray a mist of gin on all personal effects, reports.

10. Play loud Asian punk music at work station. Insist it is "easy listening."

11. Pencil in fake schedules in coworkers' planners, let boss see; e.g. "10:00: Write fan mail to Scott Wolfe."

12. Staple. Everything. Always. Because.

13. Create "I Love Hobbits" screen saver.

14. Name all of your office equipment.

15. Name all of your office equipment Mervin.

16. Leave slice of cheese in disk drive. Call Technical Support, asking why your grilled cheese isn't ready. Allow others to hear your conversation.

17. Page other people in the voice and style of the announcer in Monster Truck Rally commercials.

18. Remove clothing upon entering office. Make photocopy of outfit. Put clothes back on. File copy of outfit in notebook. Repeat daily.

19. Construct a ramshackle roof for your cubicle out of office supplies and corrugated tin.

20. Mount photo of Leonard Nimoy over desk. If anyone asks why it's there, respond, "Father." Continue working.

21. Wear swim goggles.

22. Repeatedly slide out of your chair onto the ground. Explain that you're not having a good friction day.

23. When they say, "Would you like to go to lunch?" You answer: "No thanks. I no longer consume food orally."

DO UNTO OTHERS

24. At meeting, insert pictures of Tyne Daly into slide presentation. When they come up, act shocked and defensive. Repeat at all future meetings.

25. Leave a substantially dog-eared copy of *American Psycho* at your desk.

26. Create a computer file called "Bird Fetish." Leave it conspicuously on your desk top. Fill it with doctored photos of naked men surrounded by sparrows.

27. Constantly conspire with your coworkers to run moonshine in the supplies closet.

28. Add silent b's to 60% of your words in work-related writing.

29. Have dabs of shaving cream left on your face each morning.

30. Have dabs of shaving cream left on your chest, arms, and pants each morning.

31. In the "for" space on business checks write: a) Various Gary Coleman Paraphernalia b) Ludvig's salves c) "faking the funk."

32. Stare hypnotized into your computer screen, typing nonsense, droning "I shall be avenged" over and over.

33. Order pizza to your desk. Bland, trite entry, you say? Toppings should include: dice, robin eggs, and dime size photos of Candice Bergen.

34. Include more and more fisting photographs in your reports.

35. Ask subordinates to make 500 copies of irrelevant Cosmo articles.

36. Incorporate the phrase, "Booyah" into your office vernacular.

37. When someone enters the room, break coffee mug on desk, wield it as a weapon, then say apologetically: "Sorry, thought you were Rodrigo."

38. When the boss asks for any last minute input, give a detailed account of drunken orgy with cast of White Shadow.

39. Change your voice mail to a William Shatner's spoken word version of "Rocket Man."

DO UNTO OTHERS

67

40. During a large meeting wait for someone to address you in any way. When they do, respond, shocked, "You mean you can see me?" Run out and never return.

41. Spread bizarre rumors like "there are cameras in our chairs" or "the secretaries are made of clay."

42. Replace Xerox paper with torn-out pages from the manuscript of *Palmetto*.

Index of Occupational Absurdity

Bored with your job? Here's a handy reference tool. Just find your job and read the respective spicer-upper.

Lawyer: Constantly cite precedents from "Kramer vs. Kramer," "Broncos vs. Browns," and "Joanie Loves Chachi."

Chef: Include questionable garnish: a) scrap metal b) tuft of pubic hair c) photo of Pete Harnisch.

Navy officer: Wear novelty "Fartbeat of America" underwear visible under whites.

Judge: Use your gavel to tenderize meat during trial.

Gym teacher: Teach new units a) Professional Wrestling b) Make Fun of the Nerds c) Toiling for Gems in Underground Mines.

Sportscaster: Eat a live frog on air for every home-team victory.

Teacher: Open up traditional children's story book but instead of reading the pages, politely retell episodes of MASH.

Mailman: Refuse to relinquish addressee's mail unless they beat you in Indian leg wrestling.

Actor: Upon winning the Oscar, give earnest speech, thanking a slew of pagan gods: "I'd like to thank Demeter for the bountiful harvest, and Hephaestus, without whose persistent smithing, we would not have the cutlery to consume the fruits of our harvest.

George Lucas: Include seven-minute montage of Boba Fett's failed accounting career in next *Star Wars* movie.

Governor: Make a) housing affordable b)streets safe c) Afros mandatory.

President: Change the national anthem to Quiet Riot's "Come On, Feel the Noise."

Omnipotent Deity: Make a tree that grows the heads of former Milwaukee Bucks.

Radically Rude Things to Do When Dealing With Annoying People

There are times in our lives when our patience is truly tested. Moments when, for one reason or another, we are forced to interact with the condescending, the callous, or the just plain old annoying. And it is at these times where we must muster all the tact and goodwill that dwells within us. And discard it entirely.

"These are the times that try men's souls."
—George Peppard

11 Things to Do to Get Off the Phone With a Telemarketer

1. Politely tell them, "I'm sorry. I have no free will."

2. Inquire ardently about their weight, address, sign, and "openness to new ideas."

3. Phase in and out of robotspeak.

4. If they ask, "Do you live alone?" You answer, "Do voices count?"

5. Laugh at everything they say. Sometimes break into applause.

6. Unprompted, tell them what you are wearing. Proceed to misconstrue the conversation as phone sex.

7. Speak in an indecipherable Scottish accent.

8. Assume they are your friend, Mitchell. Do not accept otherwise.

9. Refuse to cooperate unless telemarketer does a duet of "Memories" with you.

10. Answer their questions but add subtly, "Resistance is futile."

11. Claim you are in the middle of fixing your lawnmower. Provide pathetic man-made sound effects.

6 Things to Do to Annoy Alex Trebek If You're on Jeopardy

1. Phrase answers in unconventional question forms: "Is it ..."; "Would it happen to be ..."; "Do you suppose maybe it is ..."; "What in the Sam Hill is ..."

2. Say, "I'll take Jim J. Bullock to block."

3. Call Alex "Wink."

4. Buzz in for every single question and invariably answer, "Who is Merle Haggard?"

5. Write on screen during Final Jeopardy: a) I can't feel my legs b) Red Rum Red Rum Red Rum c) Up yours, Alex!

6. Answer, "What is a pompous Canadian who over-articulates?"

14 Things to Do If A Guy Is Hitting On You

1. Smell your fingers a lot.

2. Never have more than one eye open at a time.

3. Mention your current boyfriend. Mention his short temper, his Golden Gloves championship, and his rapier proficiency.

4. Mention your last boyfriend. Mention his limp, his slurred speech, and his aversion to mayonnaise.

5. Give an insufferably long-winded account of the mechanism that causes grass stains.

6. Tell them you have a tattoo. When they ask to see it, explain without a tinge of irony, "It's on the inside of my skin."

7. Talk to your breasts. Name them. Rebuke them.

8. After he says something normal, tell him you can "read between the lines" and "No, I will not practice archery with you in Korea."

9. Spill your drink. Cry like a baby.

10. Insist Paul Bunyan is real. Become enraged if he disagrees.

11. Have no control of your left hand "because of the incident."

12. Breathe extremely audibly.

13. When dancing, do not move joints and clap hands in rapid succession.

14. Take notes.

Positively Peculiar Things to Do on a First Date

The first date doesn't have to be a miserably awkward experience for both of you. At his/her expense, you can have a great time. All you have to do is use your imagination.

1. Constantly hint that you are an alien, as in "Reminds me of Zorzootz 4 . . . uh . . . I mean Venice."

2. (men) Tag on real sardonic "for a girl" to all your compliments, as in, "That skirt looks really nice on you . . . *for a girl.*"

3. Greet date with gifts: a) a stack of wrestling magazines b) your dirty laundry c) black orchids—the flower of death d) a bag of marbles and a large grouper.

4. Refuse to veer conversation away from Jacko, that Australian guy in the Energizer commercials.

5. Excuse yourself to go to the bathroom, come back sopping wet, offer no explanation.

"Love, love, nothing but love, still love, still more!
For, on love's bow Shoots buck and doe;
The shaft confounds Not that it wounds But tickles still the sore."
—"Weird" Al Yankovic

6. Eat only the parsley at dinner, lament the wasteful excessive meat and potatoes garnish.

7. Fill pants with mulch, let a little fall out from time to time, whisper, "Oh no, it's happening again."

8. Upon meeting him/her, scrape finger across his/her shoulder, taste, and say, "You'll do."

9. Wear a Members Only jacket, Jams, and a Spuds MacKenzie hat. Make references to '80's culture as if they were topical, e.g. "Have you seen that new *Pretty in Pink* movie?"

10. Greet date with the classic "Give me five, up high, down low, you're too slow."

11. Repeatedly use the word "milkweed" as an adjective, as in "This has been really milkweed."

12. Boast about your ligament strength.

13. Give her fake but believable information like: a) Paul Newman has a clubfoot, b) Frank Lloyd Wright designed this restaurant, c) Baboons are the only other species that engages in oral sex.

14. Rub hands together and smile fiendishly as you talk.

15. Two words: male perm.

16. Four words: Wear a name tag.

17. Fifteen words: Make multiple D&D references, as in "That waiter is as lawful neutral as a modron."

18. Put Parmesan cheese in your coffee.

19. When reviewing check, take out abacus, calculate with deadpan concentration.

20. Fill pockets with Russian dressing. As date eyes you, confused, explain, "For Renaldo."

21. Every time your date begins to speak, a) open up a book b) yawn c) vomit.

22. In an accusing tone, constantly compare your date unfavorably to Simon Bolivar, as in, "Simon Bolivar didn't smoke."

23. If he/she leaves for the bathroom, switch a) tables b) clothes c) hairstyle d) personality e) gender.

24. Attempt to do napkin origami. Fail. Be ruthlessly hard on yourself with "I suck!"s and "I'm such a loser!"s.

25. Order a) a fudge and ham sandwich b) gin on ground beef c) a jar of mayonnaise with cherries in it.

26. Add a "and the same for the lady/gentleman."

27. When he/she orders shake head and smirk. If they inquire what the problem is just laugh an intensely sarcastic, "No, good choice. Really."

28. Excuse yourself to go to the bathroom. Shave a little. Repeat throughout night, shaving whole body very gradually.

29. Ask for a party of three, explain to your date that your imaginary friend, "Keldin," will be joining you. Work Keldin into the conversation. Be creative.

30. Undress your date with your a) eyes b) hands c) pliers d) dwarves.

31. Have picture of golfer Craig Stadler in your wallet, stare at it with forlorn eyes, gasp, "Isn't he dreamy?"

32. Speak all your statements with an interrogative inflection?

33. Respond at entirely inappropriate times with "Is that a threat or an invitation?" or "Do the math."

34. After successfully cutting meat, exclaim proudly, "I am the shit." Do that "raise the roof" gesture.

If your date is extremely tolerant or perhaps insane, the aforementioned acts may not offend him/her. Who knows, maybe they'll even charm him/her/it into bed. If so, try these to breathe a little fire back into your love life.

1. Break into "We are the Champions" upon reaching orgasm.

2. Utter all sexual exclamations in Yiddish.

3. Say you want to get into something a little more comfortable, leave the room, come back, dressed as a) a pilgrim b) the Hamburglar c) Mark Gastineau.

4. During oral sex, mutter under your breath, "Uh, oh . . . that can't be good."

5. During intercourse, passionately shout out a) other names b) Muppets c) the members of the 1987 Milwaukee Bucks.

6. Already be wearing a condom prior to disrobing.

7. Explain that you cannot perform sexually unless witnessed by Tom Selleck. Unveil giant picture.

8. Insist on mood music: the theme to *Fame* looped over and over.

9. Insist on mood lighting—bright spotlights.

10. Insist on mood video recording: *Berry Gordy's The Last Dragon*.

11. Calmly hand her/him goggles and bag of warm spinach. Say matter-of-factly. "All right, let's get started."

12. Explain your peculiar erogenous zones: a) elbows and knees b) calves c) mahogany corner shelf in the foyer.

13. Yodel.

14. Add sensual foods to increase pleasure: hard-boiled eggs, bagel and gefilte fish, cheeseburger.

15. Hum "Ballad of the Green Berets," gradually get louder as activity becomes more intense.

16. As you get extremely excited, shout out in high-pitched robotic voice, "circuit malfunction, circuit malfunction, overload, overload, overloaaad." (Feign deactivation.)

17. After sex, remove condom and ask where she keeps the recycling bin.

18. Conduct play-by-play commentary in the voice and style of Howard Cosell.

So you've had sex . . . now: 7 Things To Do When Raising Kids

1. Write school absence notes with cut-out letters from magazines.

2. Raise your kids Pagan Greek.

3. Family pet: a) penguin b) midget c) Leonard Nimoy.

4. When they are 12, tell them you are not their natural parents. Who are? Golfing legend Lee Trevino and former British Prime Minister Margaret Thatcher.

5. Pack the same lunch every day: popcorn and a slab of cod.

6. Tell them the number 8 is against their religion and by no means are they to use it.

7. For Halloween, dress your kids as 18th Century French prostitutes.

Beautifully Bizarre Things to Do on Special Occasions

Birthday blues getting you down? Not excited by the prospects of spending an evening with the swollen graduates at your high school reunion? These are supposed to be landmark events in your life, and there are ways of making them as memorable as they are supposed to be.

"Celebrate good times . . . Let's celebrate and have a good time."
—Translated from the original German by Wagner.

5 Things to Do at a Wedding

1. Set up attacking G.I. Joe figures scaling the cake to rescue the bride. Have flankers in the punch bowl.

2. Swap tape of traditional "Here Comes the Bride" with Darth Vader's "Imperial March."

3. Wear earpiece, tell people at your table that you are a secret-service agent attached to Gerald Ford. Point to random, balding old man.

4. Show up veiled, in bridal outfit, trail behind bride, try to get them confused with the old switcheroo.

5. Bring an entourage of twelve dwarves as "your date."

5 Things to Do at a Funeral

"Death—can't live with it, can't live without it."
—Either Soren Kierkegaard or Kirk Cameron. I can't remember.

1. Motivate the pallbearers, Tony Little style.

2. Give a bogus eulogy citing fake anecdotes like the "brisket debacle" and the "time he arm-wrestled James Kahn."

3. During the eulogy, stand up and object. Claim that the prosecution is leading the witness.

4. Give a eulogy to Paula Poundstone, then shamefully admit you are in the wrong place.

5. Practice golf drives at cemetery.

5 Things to Do When Your Wife is Giving Birth

1. Encourage with excited tears, "I see it, it's beautiful," then pull out a tray of fresh-baked cookies.

2. Brag to the doctor sheepishly how all this is happening because the two of you "did it."

3. Suggest names for child: "Halibut," "Philtrum," "38," (sound of a handful of change hitting table).

4. Bring boom box, play theme from *What's Happenin'?* Say you heard it helps child development.

5. Hold baby over your head and a) insist that all bow down to their new leader b) do a set of military presses c) shout loudly, "Tonight, we feast!"

4 Things to Do at a Birthday Party

> *"At this time next year, a son will be borne unto you."*
> —Maurice Cheeks

1. Fill piñata with a) beef fat b) hot oatmeal c) live bees.

2. Forgo tired tradition of singing "Happy Birthday" for more festive Bachman Turner Overdrive hit "You Ain't Seen Nothin' Yet."

3. When offered cake, act offended, and say, "I don't eat meat, murderer!"

4. Bring inappropriate gift: a) an erotic massager b) a horse's head c) Jokey Smurf's exploding gift box. Put someone else's name on it.

5 Things to Do at a High School Reunion

1. Bring a Barbara Bush look-alike as your date.

2. Fabricate a fake career like a) professional sifter b) head of one of those dragons at Chinese parades c) postmaster general's sexual sherpa.

3. Reminisce about completely bogus fads, conspire with others. Fads include: asparagus around the neck, the silver shin craze, the boy group "The Felt Marvels."

4. Bring a non-high school friend who insists he was in your class. Dress him like a sailor.

5. Thank random people for taking your virginity and apologize for "turning into such a psychopath."

2 Things to Do If Abducted by Aliens

1. When they say, "Take me to your leader," take them to Anson "Potsie" Williams.

2. If threatened, explain that on earth all disagreements are settled by means of Riverdance duels.

4 Things to do in a Beauty Pageant

1. Special talent: throwing crabs against the wall.

2. Walk out in a sash with a fictional state on it. Examples: "Pelicia," "North Oklahoma," "Caves of Rendor."

3. Have terrible and embarrassing stains during swimsuit competition.

4. No matter what the moderator asks you during the interview portion, answer, "I am stuck on Band-aid and Band-aid's stuck on me."

3 Things to do at Sporting Events

1. Try to start unusual chants like, "Go home Carnies!" or "Put in Clooney!" or "That one came straight out of the cauldron."

2. Use giant video screen to ask for a divorce.

3. Smuggle in odd objects and walk around selling them, "Bald Caps! Get your Bald Caps!"

Some say the road experience died with Jack Kerouac. Others say it died with *Cannonball Run 2*.... We say it begins now. Some say flying is an ordeal. We say it's an opportunity. Some say the bus is for peons. We say, "What does peon mean?" In any case, whatever has you out there, be it business or pleasure or just the old travelin' bone, you want to make sure you leave your mark on the world.

> "On the road again. Just can't wait to get on the road again."
> —Pablo Picasso

10 Things to Do While on the Road

1. Attempt to initiate theological debate with toll booth attendant.

2. At a traffic light, wait till car drives up next to you, suddenly pull seat lever, plummet backward.

3. Slow to a stop next to a limousine, roll down window, ask for a) Grey Poupon b) French's mustard c) Judy Tenuta.

4. Let leash and roadkill dangle from your car.

5. Install strobe lights in headlights.

6. Add additional words to signs to make "political" statements: "STOP war," "YIELD to the Overlord," "CAUTION infidels."

7. Alter other signs: "Danger: Baldwin crossing."

8. Wave at people often, offering friendly smile. If they wave back, give an angry look and flip them the finger.

9. See how many words you can get unscrambling "Stop." This isn't funny, but you can do opts, pots, post, tops, spot. I challenge anyone to find me a 4 letter word with more anagrams. Star: arts, rats, tars. Nope. Not even close.

10. Ask passengers if they mind some music, insert taped recording of: a) Various sexual encounters b) Attempts to get homeless people to use the phrase, "Silver dollar-sized nipples" c) Endlessly repeated monotone, "God has lied, God has lied, God has lied . . ."

5 Things to Do If Pulled Over by a Cop

1. As cop approaches, stare at him confidently, wave your hand slightly, and say, "These aren't the droids you are looking for."

2. If he asks, "Do you know why I pulled you over?" You say, a) "Because of the lynx" b) "The stench of the decaying Mildred" c) "You like my groove-thing."

3. Perform pathetic attempt at hypnotism.

4. Offer him a spoonful of gravy if he'll let you go. Slyly show him the bowl in the glove compartment. Wink.

5. Explain that you have the "need for speed." Show him Medic-Alert bracelet.

5 Things to Do at a Hotel

1. Buy "Do not Disturb" style doorknob signs at novelty stores like "STAY OUT! STEREO BLASTING," "HAZARDOUS AREA: TEENAGER'S ROOM"

etc. Hang them on various doors. Better yet, create your own: "BUSY WITH MY RADISHES," "I REPEL YOUR ATTEMPTS AT MAINTENANCE," "STAY OUT. PLEASURING MYSELF WITH SOD."

2. Replace hotel soaps and shampoos with those from another hotel.

3. Leave used mint on hotel pillow with a note, "Please leave some for next guest."

4. Supplement wall decor in hotel with Menudo posters. Check out.

5. Fill trash can and entire room with husks of corn and condom wrappers.

7 Things to Do When Flying

1. Attempt to urinate in bathroom during turbulence. Contemplate as a metaphor for life.

2. Enter bathroom, exit in tattered clothes with green-dyed skin like the Incredible Hulk.

3. Dress like Mr. T. Walk through metal detector. Look incredulous when it goes off. Possibly mutter under breath, "Pity the fool."

4. Wager on plane delays.

5. Steal jokes from Seinfeld.

6. Place rocking horse on baggage carousel, ride like a merry-go-round.

7. Try to check a) a net bag of kittens b) a giant tortoise with a ribbon around it c) Tim Conway.

5 Things to Do on the Bus

1. Ask if you can see the cockpit.

2. Turn on overhead reading light. Take shirt off, oil up.

3. Take out a mirror. Touch up makeup. Make this take longer than it should. Gradually do yourself up to look like a member of Kiss.

4. For payment, offer the bus driver coupons that say "Good for one back rub" or "one be nice for a day."

5. Always look like you are about to say something to the person next to you, but don't.

4 Things to Do in Europe

1. In London, constantly cry, "This is nothing like those Crocodile Dundee movies!"

2. After learning of the French tradition of greeting each other with a kiss on the cheek inform them that, "In America, we clap our hands three times and then squeeze each other's calves."

3. Stage paintball war in Westminster Abbey.

4. Explain to English how words differ in U.S. Give examples like elevator: lift, shoes: pants, hello: please fondle me!

4 Things to Do in New York City

1. Get in background of *Today Show* camera with sign, "Willard is the father of my child."

2. Go to Elite model search open call with new looks: a) guy with plants for hands b) sopping wet guy c) "the asymmetrical look" d) the happenin' Hassid.

3. Walk through Central Park, say "Save it for the honeymoon" or "Get a room" to couples who aren't displaying the least bit of public affection.

4. Do caricatures in Central Park, spending thirty minutes in intense concentration/observation; then reveal drawings that always look exactly like Mao Tse-tung.

3 Things to Do in the Quagmire of Lakoon

1. Remove exterior spine of klatoosk, scratch back with it.

2. Bathe in Pools of Radiance, use increased power to recreate the Battle of Delnar.

3. Bottle enchanted clay off the banks of the river Sorn, mold obscene figures, cast enliven spell.

4 Things to Do If You Can Travel Through Time

1. Go to signing of Declaration of Independence, sign in very large script "Snoop Doggy Dogg," thereby forever changing the saying to "I just need your Snoop Doggy Dogg on this contract."

2. Tell Oliver Cromwell to loosen up a little.

3. Find Hitler, convince him to grow a Rollie Fingers-esque mustache so he will develop a more humorously self-effacing, light-hearted view of himself and therefore have no need to conquer the world.

4. Revise the Constitution to contain several uses of the phrase "buckwild."

More Unbelievably Unsettling Things to Do in a Job Interview

1. Challenge interviewer to arm wrestle. If it's a man, taunt him with "You got your skirt on today?" or "Why don't you take your balls out of your purse?"

2. Look at family photos on interviewer's desk and gag.

3. Incorrectly correct his/her grammar. Examples: "Between you and *I*. I don't feel *good*. My Afro *are* unkempt."

4. Stuff crotch obscenely.

5. Any time the interviewer expresses an opinion burst out derisively, "What are you, on crack-rock?"

6. Repeat everything the interviewer says. Do not stop until you repeat, "I'm calling the cops." Then run away.

7. Grab stapler, staple arm repeatedly to prove your mettle. Possibly sing "Bad, Bad Leroy Brown."

8. Periodically reintroduce yourself throughout interview.

9. Periodically reintroduce yourself as Bill Bellamy.

10. Ask your interviewer to do that thing where you each put your hands together and then you interlock your fingers with the other person and you open them up and it's like a "butthole," you know what we're talking about. That thing! When you were a kid. Everybody did it.

11. Eye dish of paper clips, ask, "Are you gonna eat that?"

12. If they ask, "Why do you wish to be a part of our firm?" You answer, a) "Because the overlord deems it necessary." b) " 'Cause Jiffy Lube's gone too commercial." c) "What firm? No one said anything about a firm."

13. Set watch alarm to go off. When it does, say, "time to re-admit Melvin," and leave.

14. Eat an entire head of lettuce during the interview.

15. If he/she sharpens a pencil, clap hands like a baby and say, "Make the sound again."

16. Wink. Again. Gradually do this more and more frequently until one eye is shut at all times.

17. In the middle of the interview, remove a contact lens and swallow it.

18. Calmly and consistently refer to your interviewer by an incorrect name such as "Wotarn." When they correct you, nod like you understand, then continue to call him/her "Wotarn."

19. Interpret every other thing they say as a come-on. Respond with, "I'm flattered, truly flattered, but I don't think this is appropriate in this situation."

20. Be extremely confident and polite, but have your balls clasped firmly at all times.

21. Attempt to sensibly incorporate the word "lozenge" into every sentence.

22. Add suffix "balls" to some of your wordballs.

23. Quote narrative actions in book, e.g., "If I might quote *The Great Gatsby*, 'Daisy walked over to the door and picked up the mail.'" Act as if a forceful point has been made.

4   Marvelously Miscellaneous Things to Do to Mess With People's Minds

Here's a potpourri of confusion-generation. Something for every occasion. A wide array of cheeky chicanery... a gumbo of hilarious hijinks,... Screw it. Here are all the leftovers.

1. Enter a leashed muskrat into a dog show.

2. Report a crime, gradually describe/correct details of perpetrator's appearance to sketch artist until he draws Burt Reynolds.

3. Supplement bland waiting-room periodicals at the dentist with hardcore porno magazines.

4. At doctor's office, substitute stool samples with Breyer's rainbow sherbert.

5. Enter spelling bee, spell every word C-H-E-W-B-A-C-C-A.

6. Take a test drive at a used-car dealership. Fill car with grass. Return and politely say you're not interested.

7. Stage bizarre cult ritual in median where Traffic Channel is filming.

8. Attend therapy: Intimate a) an attraction to Yosemite Sam b) your phobia of people named Roger c) loss of all sexual inhibition in Home Depot.

9. E-mail people totally normal e-mail articles. Claim they are from the Onion, and that they are hilarious. See if you get any response saying how funny they were.

10. On Halloween, offer kids a) a ladle full of gravy b) miniature bottles of alcohol like they have on airplanes c) Spalding Gray monologue tapes.

11. Go to fashion show, shout out bids as if the models are being auctioned.

12. Leave funny name at restaurants if there's a wait. Ideas: Pluntfarb, Sergeant Scrotie, Bigballs McGee.

13. Attend church bingo, say "You sank my battleship!" when bingo numbers are called out.

14. At bookstore, put clump of pubic hairs on page 157 of Jane Austin's *Emma*. Encourage others to do this across the world until it is the norm.

15. Write self-effacing letters to *Penthouse* Forum mentioning your "twenty-second bumblings" and your "two inches of pathetic boyhood."

16. At a Chinese restaurant, add "with Ralph Sampson" to the end of all your fortunes, i.e. "You are ready for an upswing . . . with Ralph Sampson." Other prepositional phrases to add . . . "in a big pile of brisket," "but all your loved ones will die in a violent threshing accident," "in your pants," and "in my pants."

17. Do a crazy dance at a baseball game to get on the Jumbotron. Then make yourself vomit.

18. Fill out bogus names on library cards: "Rommel," "Fishface Franklin," "Teldos, winged warrior."

19. When friend visits, get a huge piece of plywood to carry around. Set up a few native friends to hang around down the street doing the same thing. Tell your visiting friend, "That's the fad around here. Everybody's doing it."

20. Conference call . . . a) the NRA and the ACLU b) Patrick Ewing and John McLaughlin c) Bobcat Goldthwait and the pope.

21. At casino, use roulette wheel to crisp lettuce.

22. Set up your own "free samples" section at supermarkets. Sample samples: laxatives, birdseed bells, beef fat, mulch, a bowl of "candy" crickets, globs of peanut butter wrapped in fish skin. Be creative.

23. Fill friend's humidifier with a) whisky, b) urine, c) wild dingo pheromones.

24. Install the Clapper at piano recitals, ping-pong tournaments, and the musical "Stomp."

Acknowledgements

We'd like to thank our family and friends for all of their help, humor, and support. Special thanks to Jeff Sank for his prolific contributions, and to Danny Binstock and Bob Bernstein who had the idea for the job interview section, and let us use it. Thanks also to our editor, Joe Veltre, for his help and laid-back attitude and, as always, much and many thanks to our agent, Jay Mandel, without whom, we would be back working in the docks in Paraguay. Thanks to everyone else who sent us contributions and/or put up with our constant pleas for material.

About the Authors

Justin Heimberg is the author of numerous humor books including *Would You Rather...?* and *Would You Rather 2: Electric Boogaloo*, both written with David Gomberg. His humor regularly appears in various periodicals.

David Gomberg exists as a man with smoking black skin and eyes with pupils like lightening bolts. He has two large eyes and a huge nose. Gomberg has red spotted wings with a span of 40 feet. When battling large numbers of opponents he uses a set of green drums that act as *a horn of blasting* and *drums of panic* combined. He is currently a partner in an internet venture, Bunk1.com.

Contacting the Authors

To contact the authors, order additional copies of *Do Unto Others*, or read some of their other material, please visit their website at **www.sevenfooter.com**.